The Power Of Nothing

SUKHDEV VIRDEE

Copyright © 2019 Sukhdev Virdee

All rights reserved.

ISBN: 9781698660226

DEDICATION

Dedicated to the Absolute Divine
Truth That **YOU** Are!

Whole heartedly dedicated to
Lord Krishna, Lord Shiva,
Sri Ramana Maharshi and
Guru Nanak Dev Ji who have been and are
My Spiritual Guides on the path to
Self Realization and God Realization.

CONTENTS

	Acknowledgments	i
1	Introduction	1
2	Swamiji	7
3	What Is Relative Truth?	15
4	What Is Absolute Truth?	35
5	The Scriptures & Masters	47
6	What Is Nothing?	63
7	The Power Of Nothing	79
8	I Am Nothing	85
9	Questions & Answers	93
10	Extra Notes	107
11	Summary Booklet	117
12	Instructions Booklet	127
13	About The Author	137

ACKNOWLEDGMENTS

There are three friends that I have to absolutely acknowledge who knowingly or unknowingly led me to realize the Absolute Truth.

The first is Vik Sharma, the most hyperactive friend I have. He introduced me to Lord Krishna.

The second friend is Rajeev Aryan, an awakened being himself. He introduced me to the Bhagavad Gita and predicted that I would soon have a similar awakening.
This led to Self-Realization through complete surrender, love and devotion.

The third friend is Ranjan Sahu, a living encyclopedia of Spiritual Scriptures. He was sent by Lord Krishna to guide me on the path of knowledge, the Highest Truth.
This led to God-Realization through direct experiential knowledge.

INTRODUCTION

Seriously? You're interested in *nothing?* You know what *nothing* means right? Ninety-nine percent of the normal people in the world would laugh at you for spending your money and time on *nothing!*

Jokes apart, there's a very good reason for this book to be written. During my early days of listening, reading and understanding *Brahman* and *non-duality,* it didn't take me long to understand what Pure Existence or Pure Consciousness meant and to realize the fact that we (as the person) are living in an Ocean of Existence.

It took me a few months to grasp the fact that this entire Ocean of Existence cannot be experienced without Consciousness. Consciousness and Existence are inherent and inseparable. In my excitement with this realization I would speak to many people including my family and friends about the Absolute Reality being *Brahman*, which was Pure Existence Pure Consciousness.

I had never heard of the term *non-duality* till the age of forty, nor did I ever know what it meant, and that something like that was in the Upanishads. I grew up like every other kid learning that there was a Creator of the Universe that is called God. No one EVER said to me that you and God are one and the same reality.

So in my excitement after learning non-duality and the experiences of Self Realization and then God Realization, I went around telling all my friends and family about this *reality* that I and everyone else is. Not only was I telling them from my *personal* direct experience BUT it is also mentioned in the Upanishads, and almost all the great masters had spoken about it as well.

To my surprise, no one and I mean NOT A SINGLE person was even remotely interested in what I had to share. What I was experiencing was tooooooo big to keep to myself. Moreover I thought that I was helping others to transcend pain, suffering and realize that they are IMMORTAL too.

When I spoke about Pure Existence or Existence itself, Pure Consciousness or Consciousness itself, I faced a lot of flak from everyone. They ridiculed me saying that I've lost my mind and that there was nothing like Pure Existence, Brahman, True Self, and Pure Consciousness. A few who had heard some of these terms before could not believe what I was telling them about *being* one with the entire Universe and God.

The most common reply was, *"There's nothing like Pure Existence or Pure Consciousness."* This led me to think about why they all had such a reaction. Were they right by saying that it was nothing? Why were they not even willing to give it a listen, they just dismissed it as being nothing.

Science also accepts that there is Consciousness but nothing like Pure Consciousness. It accepts that things exist but there's nothing like Pure Existence. It troubled me in the beginning (and maybe you may be facing this kind of reactions from others who are not interested in even knowing what non-duality is) but I studied the word *nothing* and to my surprise and delight, everyone who said Brahman/Pure Existence is *nothing*, WAS RIGHT!

Brahman/Pure Existence is NOT A THING, so what was the harm in calling it nothing? Why did it seem offensive that someone dismissed such important knowledge as nothing?

The reason? Everybody including me knew what the word *nothing* meant BUT nobody knew what nothing IS. Upon studying the scriptures and from my own direct experience I realized that the Upanishads are actually talking about *nothing.* There is no such thing in the Universe as Brahman, Pure Existence, Pure Consciousness, Absolute Truth, Absolute Reality, Nirvana, The Tao or even God.

If all these terms and words pointed to that which is not a thing then they clearly pointed to *nothing*. Whenever we say the words, *'there is nothing,'* we always dismiss it as worthless, insignificant or non-existent. And we never pay attention to the fact that it *IS*. If *'nothing'* IS not a thing then what IS it? Because it still IS.

When you come face to face with *nothing* and inquire into it, you will find that it is *everything* that the Sages, Saints and Scriptures have spoken about for thousands of years. This is the only word in the English vocabulary that you know and yet don't know. The word *nothing* is dismissed in the material world but it is *everything* in spirituality.

Happy reading....

The
Power
Of
Nothing

THE JOURNEY:

From The Universe To GOD!

From The self To SELF!

From The Finite To INFINITE,

From The Known To UNKNOWN!

From Things To NO THINGS!

From Everything To NOTHING!

SWAMIJI

Richard scratched his head as he tried to understand something written by Swamiji in one of his latest books. It seemed like Swamiji was completely contradicting himself but he also knew that Swamiji was a spiritually enlightened being and one of the best at teaching non-duality. Richard was in a taxi that was heading towards Swamiji's ashram in Dehradun.

The cool breeze was blowing through the open car windows and Richard was excited that he was able to take a long weekend off from his hectic schedule in London. He was the number one criminal lawyer in London and serviced only elite clients as few could afford his fees.

He had had a chance to attend one of Swamiji's satsang's in the United Kingdom a few years back and had got hooked onto Swamiji's books that he bought after the satsang. He glanced at the paragraph he was reading again.

"He who knows nothing and knows that it cannot be known truly knows. He who does nothing and knows that it cannot do anything truly does. He who speaks nothing and knows that it cannot speak truly speaks. He who is nothing and knows that he is not a thing truly is."

He scratched his head again, *"What is Swamiji talking about? How is one to understand such statements?"* thought Richard to himself, as the taxi drove through the ashram gates and into an empty parking lot. A young monk dressed in a saffron robe came out of the main building and quickly helped Richard with his luggage. At the reception desk, the young monk checked him into one of the rooms and handed him the keys.

"Follow me Sir and I'll show you to your room," said the monk, as he led Richard through a narrow corridor that led to a large courtyard that had rooms in all four directions and a nice green lawn in the middle.

They reached the room and the monk opened the lock and placed Richard's luggage in the room. *"It's quite chilly, I hope you have some warm clothes. If you require anything you can press that bell button and someone will attend to you. It's almost dinnertime and in an hour we'll be serving dinner at the lawn. You'll have the chance to meet other seekers like yourself and mingle around with them. Oh and Swamiji will be joining us after dinner. Thank you sir,"* said the monk as he closed the door behind him.

Richard looked around the room. *"Hmmm...Quite a simple room with just the basic amenities,"* thought Richard, as he unpacked his suitcase. He quickly had a hot shower and freshened up. He was excited to be at the ashram and to meet Swamiji, even if it was for just two nights.

"What can I learn in just two nights? I guess it's better than not meeting him at all. Can I become spiritually enlightened by his mere presence or glance?" These were the thoughts running through Richard's mind when suddenly he heard a loud gong. He got up and opened the door.

"Sir, dinner is served, please proceed to the lawn," said another monk as he hurriedly passed Richard. He was knocking on every room and informing the guests that dinner was served.

Richard locked his door and walked out into the lawn where a buffet had been laid out. A few tables with chairs had also been laid out and slowly some people started trickling into the lawn. In about ten minutes there were around thirty people in total that had queued up in a line to be served dinner.

David looked around at all the people as some sat at the round tables with steaming plates of food. *"Strange! There's not a single Indian person here. Everyone here seems to be of European origin,"* thought Richard, as he filled his plate with food. It was all vegetarian but both Indian and Western delicacies were being served.

He sat at a table with five other people. *"Hi there, my name is Peterson. I'm French and this is my wife Debbie,"* said a well-groomed man in his sixties wearing a grey western suit and round glasses. *"Hi, I'm Richard. I'm from London where I practice law,"* replied Richard with a smile, *"London huh? I lived there for a few years before we moved to France. When did you get here and how did you know about Swamiji?"* asked Peterson.

"Well I just arrived a couple of hours ago. I attended Swamiji's satsang in the UK and have been drawn to his teachings about non-duality ever since. I had written to the ashram asking for some time to come and visit Swamiji and after two years they wrote back asking if I would like to visit this weekend, so I took up the offer and boarded the next flight to India. How about you guys? Been here for long?" asked Richard.

"Nah. We arrived this morning as well. We received a similar email and couldn't miss out on such an opportunity," replied Peterson. Everyone at the table introduced themselves to each other and Richard realized that this was a special two nights meeting with Swamiji arranged for a few select people from Europe. He was one of the fortunate ones to receive an email from the ashram.

Once dinner was over a couple of monks quickly put away all the tables and arranged all the chairs to face a small stage that had a single chair facing the rest of them. A sound system had been set up too. A monk took to the microphone and spoke in an impressive British accent.

"Ladies and gentlemen please be seated. I'd like to welcome each and every one of you to Swamiji's ashram. We hope you had your dinner. Swamiji will be joining us soon and I can assure you that Swamiji's talk will go on for a few hours. He likes to have his talks post midnight. Make sure you have warm clothes as it will become very cold later on."

"This satsang has been organized specially for Swamiji's many devotees and followers who live in Europe. Swamiji himself selected whom he wanted to invite and so there must be something special in each and every one of you here tonight. We'll have a tea break at two thirty and breakfast will be served at five thirty in the morning."

"No recordings of these talks will be allowed even on your mobile phones but you may take down any notes you like. A notepad and pens will be distributed soon. We ask you to maintain silence when Swamiji is speaking and refrain from interfering while he talks. Swamiji will conduct the satsang tonight and tomorrow night. You'll find that most of your questions will be answered as Swamiji talks. However feel free to note down your questions for the Q & A session tomorrow night. You will be able to ask Swamiji any questions that you may still have."

"One last request. Swamiji neither condemns nor promotes any religion and we ask you to refrain from mentioning any religious rituals, practices or questions related to any specific religion. Every religion has spirituality at its core but spirituality itself has no religion. Please refrain from asking about domestic and personal matters as well. Spirituality is about 'you' and Swamiji welcomes any questions pertaining to 'you'. Thank you very much and Swamiji will be joining us soon," said the monk, as he walked off the stage.

A couple of musicians with a hand drum and acoustic guitar who were seated on one side of the stage began to play some soothing soulful music. One of them sang some beautiful mantras after which she broke into the English rendition of *Amazing Grace* and while she had everyone mesmerized with her voice, Swamiji walked onto the stage and took his seat, put on and adjusted his wireless headset microphone. He gazed at everyone starting from his right side panning all the way to the left.

A few people already had tears running down their cheeks. Richard was seated right in the front row and he had a great view of Swamiji. When the song was over the musicians quickly got up and left to sit at the back. Swamiji spoke in a deep and soothing velvety voice.

"Welcome to satsang. 'Sat' means the absolute truth and 'sang' means 'association with' or 'in the company of'. Thus satsang means association with or in the company of the absolute truth. That is what we will be talking about tonight."

"I'm sure that most of you have read many different philosophies regarding God, the Absolute Truth, Absolute Reality, Brahman, Nirvana, the Tao Te Ching that are absolutely great and I have a very high regard for them but tonight I want us to discuss and talk about only the truth, the Absolute Truth and nothing else."

"We will talk a lot of common sense and not throw around big words that you may have read somewhere before. We are going to talk about 'you' and your day-to-day experience. Experiences that are common to every human being on earth that we may have not paid attention to or understood at all because life got in the way."

"So I'm not going to be talking about anything that's beyond what you already know and experience. You may find nothing new in what we talk, but please feel free to note down any questions as they arise in your mind. It's only a two nights talk and either these two nights may change you forever before you leave or maybe a few months or years down the line, but I promise you that if you pay attention to what I will be saying, a 'seed' will be planted in your mind and the one who waters that seed regularly will surely and eventually see a huge tree in place of that tiny seed. So, I request you to please listen attentively and make a note of any questions you have. Great let's begin," said Swamiji in his deep velvety and authoritative but soothing voice.

WHAT IS RELATIVE TRUTH?

Swamiji continued, *"I said that we'd be talking about the Absolute Truth and nothing else. I'll begin with what the two words mean. The word 'Absolute' means accurate, complete, pure or unalloyed in any way. And the word 'truth' means that which is a fact or real. So when I say the 'Absolute Truth', it means the accurate, complete, pure and unalloyed truth/fact/reality."*

"We already know many truths, facts and realities. For example the fact that we are all in Dehradun, I am talking, you are wearing warm clothes, you travelled from your respective country to be here etc. You know your gender, your names, where you live, your family, what you learnt at school and college etc."

"You also know that you are sitting on a chair right now, your internal feelings, desires, emotions and thoughts. All these are plain and simple facts, truths and realities that we are completely sure of in our minds."

"So, is the fact that we are in Dehradun NOT the absolute truth? We know it is the truth BUT is it or isn't it the Absolute Truth? If it is the Absolute Truth then we are spiritually enlightened and have realized what all the Sages and Saints of the past have spoken about again and again."

"But if it is NOT the Absolute Truth, and yet we still know it to be the truth, then what KIND of truth is it? It must be some OTHER kind of truth."

"Well the fact that we are in Dehradun is true but so is the fact that it is night time right now. You know your name is also true. If we believe this to be true, then there are many such facts, truths and realities in the Universe. All these facts, truths and realities are about many different things, in many different places and at many different times. And these facts or truths also keep changing constantly."

"This is what we have all learnt about at school, college, from friends, parents, elders and life in general. This is what we know to be the truth in our lives. This is NOT the Absolute Truth, and I'll explain why as we go along BUT let's first understand what kind of truth/fact/reality THIS ONE is."

"Everything that we know for a fact, as the truth or real is known as 'relative' truth, 'relative' reality or 'relative' fact. The word 'relative' means in relation/comparison/proportion to something else. Thus the fact or truth that we are seated in Dehradun is 'relatively' true when compared to the other truth known as 'absolute' truth."

"There are millions and billions of such relative truths, facts or realities, but how can we figure out what determines something to be 'relatively' true or 'absolutely' true?"

"Anything that is limited in time, space and object identity is 'relatively' true. What does that mean? Any thing/object in the Universe that is either, then or when (limited in time), here or there (limited in space), or this or that (limited as an object), is only 'relatively' true. The entire Universe qualifies to be 'relatively' true. Everything in the Universe is 'relatively' true or 'relatively' real. The Universe is 'relatively' true or 'relatively' real."

"Yet we don't feel that way about ourselves or the Universe. We feel that everything before us is real since we can have a first hand experience of the things around us. We can see, hear, smell, taste and touch many things and therefore they cannot be negated as being unreal, illusions, appearances etc."

"We know the world and Universe to be as real as we are. The fact that we are alive cannot be unreal. Just as we are alive and real so is the Universe. But what we currently think and know our self to be is also only 'relatively' true. We feel that we are the body and mind, that we were born and will die, that we are either here or there, that we are our self only and not anything or anybody else. Just like everything else in the Universe is only 'relatively' true, so are we (as the person)."

"Anything that is seen, heard, tasted, smelt or touched is only relatively true."

"Anything that is thought, imagined, dreamt, visualized, remembered or understood is also only relatively true."

"Anything that is known or unknown is only relatively true."

"Anything that is perceived or experienced by the five senses and/or the mind is only relatively true."

"Everything that 'exists' is only relatively true. Everybody that 'exists' is only relatively true."

"Everything in the Universe is only relatively true. The Universe as we know it is only relatively true."

"Is there a way of knowing everything in the Universe? Certainly there is! If you know what glass is, then you know every thing that is made of glass. The things/objects may have different names and forms, be located in different parts of the world and exist at different times, but by knowing what glass is, you know the substance or the reality of everything glass."

"If you know what iron is then you know the substance or reality of everything iron. In the same way if you knew what a 'thing' is then you would know everything in the Universe."

"The Universe is made up of trillions of different things, but they're all 'things' nevertheless. Do you know anything that is NOT a thing? It's not possible, the words 'everything' and 'anything' themselves contain the word 'thing'."

"Everything that you know is a thing, either a PHYSICAL thing in the Universe that you can see, hear, smell, taste or touch OR a MENTAL thing in your mind that you know, think, imagine, feel, desire, emote or dream."

"The Universe is made up of 'things'. They could be physical (tangible) or mental (intangible) things, but they are all 'things' that can be EXPERIENCED or PERCEIVED by the mind."

Universe = Things

"Let's us understand what a 'thing' is. A 'thing' is that which you can experience or perceive with your five senses and/or mind."

*"A 'thing' is that which is **limited in time, space and object identity.** A thing is that which has a specific **name, form and use.**"*

*"A 'thing' is that which you are **'aware' of.** A 'thing' is that which you are **'conscious' of.**"*

"Anything and everything that you perceive or experience must be 'apart' or 'separate' from you."

*"Whatever you see, hear, smell, taste or touch must be 'apart' or 'separate' from you. This covers all the things **'external'** to your body. It covers all the **physical** or **tangible** things."*

*"Whatever you think, understand, know, imagine, feel, dream, visualize or desire must also be 'apart' or 'separate' from you. This covers all the **'internal'** things in your mind. It covers all the **mental** or **intangible** things."*

*"All 'things' tangible and intangible, physical and mental are experienced or perceived in your mind in the form of **'thought'.**"*

"Everything in the Universe is experienced or perceived by you in the form of different 'thoughts' in the mind."

"'Things' are experienced or perceived by your mind only in the form of 'thought'. Whatever you see, hear, smell, taste, touch, think, understand, know, imagine, feel, dream, visualize or desire is reduced to being only a thought."

Things = Thoughts

"So far we have reduced the entire infinite Universe to that which are called 'things'. The Universe is made up of trillions of different and separate 'things'."

"All these 'things' are experienced or perceived by your mind in the form of 'thoughts'. A 'thing' is only a 'thought' in your mind. As many 'things' that you know, that many 'thoughts' in your mind. Of course only one thought can be experienced at a time by your mind. You cannot think two or more thoughts simultaneously. It's possible to think of multiple things in the same thought but you can't have more than one thought at a time."

Universe = Things
Things = Thoughts
A Million Things = A Million Thoughts

"Life is only one continuous experience from birth to death. Since every 'thing' in the Universe is experienced or perceived in the form of thoughts, and thoughts arise and subside only in the mind, we can conclude that you experience your life 'IN' the mind only. Your life is experienced in the mind only in the form of continuous thoughts."

Universe = Things
Things = Thoughts
Thoughts = Experience
Experience = Mind
Mind = Your Life!

Your *'Life'* Is Simply Your *'Mind'* That *'Experiences'* Continuous *'Thoughts'* About *'Things'* In The *'Universe!'*

Your *'Mind'* Experiences Your *Life!*

Your *Life* Is Experienced *'IN'* Your *Mind!*

"Everything in the Universe is only a thing. And a thing is only a thought in the mind. Thus the Universe, a person and the person's experience of life in the Universe are all only 'relative' truth. We have qualified everything in the Universe as 'relative' truth, which means that there should be a higher truth that is truer or more real than everything and everybody in the Universe."

"This is what the Sages and Saints, and all the Spiritual Scriptures talk about. They refer to it with different names which we will go through later but if this is clear then we can move on to understand this higher truth or higher reality that is complete, accurate, pure, unalloyed and ABSOLUTE," said Swamiji, looking at everyone. Nobody seemed to be confused about this so far. It also seemed like a lot of common sense.

It was past one o'clock in the morning and the moon was shining brightly. It was getting quite cold now and the monks had lit up a few small fires on the sides to keep the guests warm.

Swamiji took a few slow sips of water from the glass placed on his side table. A few of the seekers were quickly jotting down notes from what Swamiji had just explained. Richard flipped the pages on his notepad to see what he had noted down.

> Everything That We Know For A Fact, As The Truth Or Real Is Known As 'Relative' Truth, 'Relative' Reality Or 'Relative' Fact!

Anything That Is Limited In Time, Space & Object Identity Is 'Relatively' True!

> What We Currently Think And Know Ourselves To Be Is Also Only 'Relatively' True!

> Everything That Exists Is Only Relatively True!
>
> Everybody That Exists Is Only Relatively True!
>
> The Universe As We Know It Is Only Relatively True!

If You Know What Glass Is, Then You Know Everything That Is Made Of Glass!

If You Know What A 'Thing' Is, Then You Would Know Everything In The Universe!

Everything That You Know Is A 'Thing'!

Either
A PHYSICAL Thing In The Universe
OR
A MENTAL Thing In Your Mind!

THE UNIVERSE = THINGS!

A Thing Is That Which Has A Specific Name, Form And Use!

A Thing Is That Which You Are AWARE Of!

A Thing Is That Which You Are CONSCIOUS Of!

All 'THINGS'
Tangible
And Intangible,
Physical & Mental
Are
Experienced
Or Perceived
In Your Mind
In The Form
Of
THOUGHT!

THINGS = THOUGHTS!

Universe = Things
Things = Thoughts
Thoughts = Experience
Experience = Mind
Mind = Your Life!

Your LIFE Is
Simply Your MIND That
'Experiences'
Continuous
THOUGHTS
About THINGS
In The
Universe!

WHAT IS ABSOLUTE TRUTH?

"Should we carry on?" asked Swamiji and everyone shouted a resounding, *"YES!"* *"Great! What we have spoken of so far must be sheer common sense that cannot be refuted in any way. It comprises of your daily experiences."*

"What we are going to talk about now may seem ridiculous but if you follow what I say carefully it will seem quite **SIMPLE to understand but IMPOSSIBLE to be.** *So please pay attention and don't forget to take notes for reference."*

"The Absolute Truth or Absolute Reality is that truth that is complete, accurate, pure, unalloyed and absolute. We defined relative truth to be, that which is limited in time, space and object identity. Basically everything in the Universe including what we know ourselves to be is all 'relative' truth."

"This means that everything in the entire Universe including the person that we think and know ourselves to be is NOT the Absolute Truth."

"We cannot see the Absolute Truth with our eyes. We cannot hear the Absolute Truth with our ears. We cannot smell, taste or touch the Absolute Truth with our nose, tongue and skin. We cannot think of the Absolute Truth. We cannot imagine, dream, remember or understand the Absolute Truth. Basically, we cannot experience or perceive the Absolute Truth with either our body or our mind."

"We have just negated everything that you can think, say or do, everything and everybody in the Universe as NOT the Absolute Truth. What is left if we negate the entire Universe as NOT the Absolute Truth? Nothing! So, is the Absolute Truth nothing?"

*"Let's take a look at WHAT is the Absolute Truth or Absolute Reality. If the 'relative' truth is limited in time, space and object identity, then the Absolute Truth or Absolute Reality should be that which is **NOT limited in time, space and object identity.**"*

"If the Absolute Truth is NOT limited in time, then it has no beginning, middle or end, it never came into existence, existed or went out of existence, it was never created, preserved or destroyed, it was never born, lived or died. That which is NOT limited in time is called Eternal, Timeless or Immortal. **The Absolute Truth is that which is Eternal, Timeless and Immortal.**"

"If the Absolute Truth is NOT limited in space, then there is no space or place in the Universe that it is not. It is here, there and everywhere SIMULTANEOUSLY. That which is NOT limited in space is called OMNIPRESENT. **The Absolute Truth is Omnipresent.**"

"And if the Absolute Truth is NOT limited by object identity, then there is no object or thing in the Universe that it is not. It is this thing, that thing and everything. This includes all the physical (tangible) and mental (intangible) things. That which is NOT limited object identity is called NON-DUAL. There is nothing apart from the Absolute Truth. **The Absolute Truth is Non-dual** *(One without a second)."*

*"So the Absolute Truth or Absolute Reality is Immortal, Omnipresent and Non-dual. If every 'thing' is the 'relative' truth and a 'thing' is that which has a name, form and use, then the Absolute Truth or Absolute Reality should be that which has no name, no form and no use. **The Absolute Truth is that which is Nameless, Formless and Useless** (The Absolute Truth cannot be used for anything)."*

*It is ONE entity that **transcends** and **unifies** the entire Universe **simultaneously**. It transcends everything and unifies everything as itself. It transcends all 'relative' truths and unifies all of them as **ONE Absolute Truth.** It is higher, truer and more real than anything your mind knows in the Universe."*

*"The Absolute Truth can also be said to be truly **infinite**, that which is absolutely limitless in any way possible. Do we know of any such thing or entity in the world or Universe? No, we already negated every 'thing' whether physical or mental. There is no such thing in the Universe that is everywhere, every time and everything. The universe itself is infinite but we don't experience or perceive it as one entity. It seems divided into different and separate things that are limited in time and space."*

"The Absolute Truth sounds like an IMPOSSIBLE entity. There is nothing such as the Absolute Truth or Absolute Reality the way we have just heard it to be. It is impossible and non-existent in the Universe. The Absolute Truth as described does NOT exist in the Universe. It is nowhere, never and nothing. There is nothing like the Absolute Truth or Absolute Reality. The Absolute Truth is NOTHING!"

"In the absence of this Absolute Truth or Absolute Reality, we feel and know the 'relative' truth to be the only truth and fact. This is because we can confirm it with our senses and mind. We can see, hear, smell, taste, touch and think of these 'relative' truths."

"So, this Absolute Truth is not something that can be proven to exist, it is non-existent. How can our mind know or understand it if it does not exist? It can't! One way we can approach this is to 'believe' or have 'blind faith' that it IS, even though it is nothing and doesn't exist. We can 'believe' and have 'blind faith' in the teachings and pointing's of the enlightened Sages and Saints who claim that they know it, and that it cannot be known (paradoxical and contradicting words). This is the God approach."

"The other way is to inquire for ourselves using the teachings and pointing's of the enlightened masters. This approach is known as Self-Inquiry. We'll take a look at both these approaches after a short tea break. I'm sure you must be feeling the cold by now and a hot cup of tea or coffee would be good at this point. Let's take a break of twenty minutes and when we come back we'll take a look at what all the past enlightened masters pointed to in their teachings," said Swamiji, as he got up, took off the headset microphone and came off the stage.

Everyone got up and headed towards the long table on the side where a couple of monks were serving tea, coffee, cookies, cheese sandwiches and some Indian snacks that included *samosas* and *bhajias*.

A few others were still seated scribbling on their notepads and Richard finished his last note and flipped back to read what he had written.

The
Absolute Truth
Or
Absolute Reality
Is That Truth
That Is Complete,
Accurate, Pure,
Unalloyed
And Therefore
Absolute!

Everything
In The Entire
Universe
Including
The Person That
We Think And
Know Ourselves
To Be Is

NOT

The
Absolute Truth!

> The Absolute Truth Or Absolute Reality IS That Which Is NOT LIMITED In Time, Space And Object Identity!

> The Absolute Truth Or Absolute Reality IS That Which **IS** Timeless, Omnipresent & Non-Dual!

> We CANNOT Experience Or Perceive The Absolute Truth With Our Body OR Our Mind!

The
Absolute Truth
Does NOT Exist
In The Universe!
It Is Nowhere;
Never And Is
Not A Thing.

There Is Nothing
Like The
Absolute Truth!

The
Absolute Truth Is
NOTHING!

THE SCRIPTURES & MASTERS

Everyone mingled with each other as they relished the Indian snacks and hot *chai*. Swamiji was right there with them, greeting and talking to a few of them. Some people stood next to the fires that were lit to warm their hands.

The lawn was well lit up and a peacock, a couple of squirrels and green parrots could be seen moving about in the trees. Once everyone was done with the tea and coffee, Swamiji went back up onto the stage and wore his headset microphone and within a few minutes everyone else had taken his or her seats waiting for Swamiji to continue.

"We'll take a look at what the spiritually enlightened masters spoke about. What did they try to teach the rest of the people who were around them? What do the ancient spiritual scriptures talk about?"

"Most of the major religions around the world speak of a God who created this entire Universe. A God who is all powerful, omniscient, omnipotent, omnipresent, all forgiving, kind, caring, loving, just etc. None of the religions have been able to 'prove' the existence of that God."

"They cannot point to something or anything in the Universe and claim, 'that is the God we are talking about'. The God of religion cannot be seen, heard, smelt, tasted, touched or thought and understood by the mind. Why? Because we have already seen that there is no entity in the Universe that is everywhere, every time and in everything as the God of religion is usually claimed to be."

"I'm not saying that they are wrong, what I want us to understand is that all these teachings and pointing's about God point to nothing in the Universe. The Universe is made of things and things are experienced as thoughts BUT God is not a thing. God does NOT exist like other things in the Universe and therefore our mind cannot experience or perceive God. If God is everywhere, every time and in everything, then He/She/It should also be here, now and in anything that you choose to see or touch."

"No religion can point out God in the chair that you are sitting on, or the tea and coffee that we just had. And if God is NOT in the chair or the tea and coffee or any other thing here and now, then the claim of being everywhere, every time and in everything is false. Either the claim is false or the understanding of God presented is incomplete. I'll talk about this again later. For now it is simple that we cannot see God because He/She/It is not a thing and this Universe is entirely made up of existing things, both tangible and intangible. God is not a thing. God is nothing."

"Then we have the other kind of scriptures or teachings and pointing's such as the Upanishads that don't even acknowledge a separate entity called God. They talk about 'you' as being the 'absolute truth' or the 'absolute reality'. They talk about human beings being 'ignorant' about their real identity. They say that the seeker thinks himself or herself to be the body and the mind and that that is the problem and the cause of all fear, pain and suffering."

"The Upanishads say that you are not the body, not the breath or life force within the body, not the mind, not the intellect and not even the blank darkness beyond the intellect. If you are NOT any of those then what or who are you? The Upanishads claim that you are 'Brahman'. What or who is this Brahman? Brahman is defined as existence, consciousness infinite.

"Brahman is infinite Pure Existence and Pure Consciousness. We saw what the word 'infinite' means. That which is not limited in time, space or object identity. What is Pure Existence? We know of things that exist or things that have existence in them. Pure existence would mean existence without a thing. There is no thing in the Universe that is known as Pure Existence. Existence cannot be separated from a thing. Therefore Pure Existence is not a thing. It doesn't exist. **Pure Existence is nothing!"**

"Let's take a look at Pure Consciousness in the same way. We know we are conscious of many different things including our body, mind and the world around us BUT Pure Consciousness means Consciousness without things (tangible or intangible). As long as you are awake, you are conscious of your body, your mind and the surroundings that you are in. When you go to sleep and dream, you are conscious of dream body, dream mind and dream world."

"In deep sleep, the scientists will say there is no consciousness while the Upanishads will say there is only consciousness. Either way, what is YOUR personal experience of deep sleep? It was blank and there was nothing. I slept soundly without any disturbance. There was no physical or mental thing/object that you were conscious of in deep sleep. There was nothing. Pure Consciousness is not a thing. There is no thing called Pure Consciousness. **Pure Consciousness is nothing!"**

"Brahman of the Upanishads is actually referring to nothing! Other words used in scriptures to describe or point to the Absolute Truth are Absolute Reality, Nirvana, Non-Duality, Pure Bliss, Supreme Being, the Creator and Tao. None of them is a 'thing' that exists in the Universe (tangible or intangible). All of them point towards one word in the English dictionary which is NOTHING!"

Absolute Truth
Absolute Reality
Brahman
Nirvana
True Self
Pure Existence
Pure Consciousness
Pure Bliss
Supreme Being
The Tao
God
The Creator.

None of the above is a *thing* that *exists* in the Universe.
All the above terms point to *NOTHING!*

"Some Sages and Saints taught that God is the Absolute Truth and Absolute Reality while another set of enlightened masters taught that YOU are the Absolute Truth/Reality. Both are talking about NOTHING! GOD is nothing and YOU are nothing. The problem with God is that no one has ever proven the existence of God."

"Hence if you follow the teachings of the masters who spoke about God, you will have to start off with blind 'faith' and 'belief' in the existence of God. This kind of foundation is easily shaken when things go wrong in life and your blind faith and belief doesn't seem to be working. Also if someone asked you about God, you wouldn't be able to give him or her a speck of proof of the existence of God."

"If you follow the teachings of the Self-Inquiry masters who say that YOU are the Absolute Truth/Reality, there is definitely one big major advantage and that is that you can never doubt your own existence. You exist is a fact to you and need not be doubted in any way. The existence of God can be doubted BUT the fact that YOU exist cannot be doubted. You have to exist to even doubt it."

"The problem in Self-Inquiry is that, I know as a matter of fact that I exist BUT I am facing ALL the problems in life. God may or may not exist BUT God has no problems, He/She/It is all-powerful. I definitely exist BUT I have ALL the problems.

GOD:
God Has NO Problems
BUT
God's Existence Is DOUBTFUL.

SELF-INQUIRY:
I Exist BEYOND DOUBT
BUT
I Have ALL The Problems.

*"Here's what we do at this ashram. We take **your** definite undoubted existence and God's 'no problems' and put them together. You do NOT need to start with blind faith and belief AND you do NOT need have all the problems. We eliminate the disadvantages of both approaches and combine the advantages of both."*

"This is non-duality. You and God are one and the same entity; your mind just doesn't know it. Your mind is ignorant of your true identity as being the same as God's. Your mind doesn't know it because it can't know it. Remember both God and You are NOTHING! Let's inquire into what we 'think' or 'know' ourselves to be.

"Every human being says 'I am so and so'

or 'I am this and that'. For example I am Swamiji, but before I am Swamiji, I am. What is the 'I am' that every person claims to be? 'I am' simply means that I exist. I must exist before I am Swamiji. 'I am' refers and points to nothing. If you said 'I am' and stopped there, would anyone know what or who you are? No. You exist AS something or somebody. Just 'I am' on its own means nothing to anyone in the world. The words you put after 'I am' define what or who you are in the world (the person). I am a doctor would mean you exist as a doctor. The word 'doctor' would define you (the person). 'I am' doesn't define you at all. 'I am' on its own means nothing."

"God is nothing and your 'I Am' is also nothing. God and 'I Am' is the same entity, nothing. In fact from what we've seen so far, we can conclude the following:

Absolute Truth is NOTHING!
Absolute Reality is NOTHING!
Brahman is NOTHING!
Pure Existence is NOTHING!
Pure Consciousness is NOTHING!
Pure Bliss is NOTHING!
Nirvana is NOTHING!
God is NOTHING!
'I Am' is also NOTHING!

"This much information is enough for tonight. I wanted you all to understand that everything that we know is 'relatively' true compared to the 'absolute truth'. The absolute truth is NOTHING! All the scriptures, masters and teachings ALL point to NOTHING! It would be pointless to waste your time and effort in search of the Absolute Truth, God, Your True Self or Brahman anywhere, anytime in anything in the Universe (tangible or intangible)."

"God/Brahman/Self/Absolute Truth does NOT exist in this Universe. This much information should put an end to any search that you may have embarked on to find the Absolute Truth, Brahman, Your True Self or God. It cannot be found because it is non-existent and not a thing. ***IT IS NOTHING!"***

"The sun will be up in a few minutes. I'll stop here but later on tonight we shall inquire into what is nothing, your 'I am', and the power of nothing. Please have breakfast before you go to your rooms. I will see you all later on tonight," said Swamiji as he took off his headset microphone and walked off stage and towards one of the rooms in the ashram. Richard quickly finished jotting down the important points on his notepad.

GOD Can Never Be Proven To Exist Because GOD, Like The Absolute Truth Is Also Everywhere, Every Time & In Everything!

We Cannot See
God Because
He/She/It
Is Not A Thing!
The Universe Is
Made Up Of
Existing Things,
Both Tangible
And Intangible!

God Is Not
A Thing!

God Is
NOTHING!

Brahman Is
Defined As
Pure Existence
Pure Consciousness
Infinite!

No Thing Is
Infinite!

Pure Existence Is
Not A Thing!

Pure Consciousness
Is Not A Thing!

> Pure Existence Is NOTHING!
>
> Pure Consciousnes Is NOTHING!
>
> No 'Thing' Is Infinite!
>
> Infinity Is NOTHING!
>
> Brahman Is NOTHING!

All The Scriptures Sages And Saints Talk About That Which Is NOT A THING!

They Are Talking About NOTHING!

Absolute Truth, God, Brahman, Real Self, Freedom etc. IS NOTHING!

Either You Are Seeking GOD Or You Are Seeking Your True Self!

BOTH ARE NOTHING!

You Are Seeking NOTHING!

You Have To
Go From:

The Finite
To
The Infinite!

The Known
To
The Unknown!

Everything
To
NOTHING!

WHAT IS NOTHING?

Richard slept like a baby throughout the day. He had arrived the previous day and wasn't expecting to be up all night for a talk with Swamiji. Most of the seekers who were invited too stayed in their rooms almost all day long.

The staff was kind enough to serve everyone breakfast and lunch in their rooms. Just a few people did manage to get out of the ashram to explore the city before returning back in the afternoon for lunch, relaxing and napping before dinnertime.

At eight o'clock sharp the gong for dinner was sounded. Richard got up from his bed to answer the knock on his door. The monk at the door politely said, *"Sir, dinner is served, please proceed into the lawn,"* before hurrying on to the next door.

Richard placed Swamiji's book on the bed that he had been reading, locked the door behind him and walked into the lawn. This time he had enough time to look around and appreciate what was going on.

He realized that the food prepared consisted of both Western and Indian delicacies. The staff comprising of a few monks spoke English very well, and were very polite and respectful to every guest. They wore a smile on their faces all the time and seemed to be enjoying looking after the guests.

The lawn was quite big and square, having soft grass all over. At the edges of the lawn were a few trees that were home to many birds and squirrels. The peacock walked around the lawn completely undisturbed by the presence of so many people.

The guests comprised of couples and singles, all from Europe. Their age ranged from early twenties to early seventies. Richard picked up a plate and some cutlery at the buffet table where a couple of monks were serving the food. He was surprised to see different kinds of salads, pasta, lasagna, sandwiches and soup as part of the buffet, apart from the popular Indian *biryani, daal, chapatti, paneer masala, papad and butter naans.*

Richard filled his plate with a little of both and sat at a round table where already two couples were having their food. One of the couples was in their mid forties and were from Portugal while the other couple was in their late fifties and had come from Germany.

Richard introduced himself and they all got talking, laughing and sharing their stories of how they came to know about Swamiji, their life experiences back home and general chit chat about life. Most of them had either attended Swamiji's satsang's in Europe or read one of his books, which drew them towards learning more from Swamiji.

After dinner was over the monks picked up all the tables and set up the chairs exactly like they were the night before. It would still be about an hour before midnight, and before Swamiji would come and give his talk.

Richard took this opportunity to introduce himself and make friends with many of the other guests. While taking to them, he realized how true Swamiji was when he said that mostly people are either searching for God or searching for their own true Self.

Even though both paths led to the same realization, the difference was in the attitude of the people who chose either path. Some believed in that higher power and acknowledged that they (as the person) were nothing compared to God. They had surrendered themselves to God even though they had never seen or known God.

The other set of people wanted to know the truth about themselves, they knew somewhere in the back of their minds that they are more than just a body and mind, that they had something higher to achieve than the usual common goals of earning a living, working, getting married, raising children, retiring and waiting for death.

Swamiji had attracted both kinds of seekers that seemed to be going in opposite directions. *"Amazing,"* thought Richard to himself, *"I want to find God. I want to find my true Self. And Swamiji says that everyone who either found God or his or her true Self found that it was the same one entity that was given different names such as Brahman, Nirvana, Freedom, Liberation, God, Self, Tao, Pure Consciousness, Pure Existence, Sat-Chit-Ananda, Pure Bliss etc."*

"And if we look at all these words and terms given to us (by the Sages and Saints who did realize God or their true Self) from the common man's or the scientist's point of view, they all refer to nothing. It is so true! Every time I've tried talking to someone about Pure Consciousness or Pure Existence, I've been told there's nothing like that."

"If any of these words did mean something, the scientists would be the first to take it into the laboratory and dissect it. None of the words given by the spiritually enlightened Saints refer to a thing. A thing is an object and object can be studied and analyzed by science. What can a scientist do 'to' nothing? What can a scientist do 'with' nothing? He can't reduce it to being an object. No wonder science will never find God or the True Self, because it is not an object but the Subject of all objects in the Universe." Light bulbs were going on in Richards mind as he thought all this.

Swamiji walked onto the stage precisely at midnight and there was pin drop silence. Swamiji sat on his chair, wore his microphone, took a sip of water and cleared his throat before he spoke.

"Welcome everyone. I hope you caught up with sleep during the day. It's been over thirty years and I still prefer the nighttime for my talks. Last night we saw that all the things that mankind knows are only 'relatively' true when compared to the 'absolute truth', which is only ONE (non-dual). Tonight we'll look at what nothing actually is. I'm sure no one here has ever been taught about nothing. When was the last time you 'looked' for nothing? When was the last time you paid 'attention' to nothing?"

"You may know what nothing means but can you see nothing, hear nothing, touch nothing, smell nothing, taste nothing, think nothing, remember nothing, imagine nothing? If you did any of those I'd love to hear what it was like. If you can see nothing, what is it like? If you can think nothing, what is it like? We'll take a look at 'nothing' from the beginning, don't forget to take down notes, you may surprise yourself later on," said Swamiji looking at everyone.

"Right, so what is nothing? 'Nothing', is defined by various English dictionaries in the form of a pronoun as; not anything, no thing, not a single part of something, non-existent, zero, that which has no importance or substance, insignificant or worthless. These are a few of the different definitions of the word 'nothing'. And they're all very true."

"Nothing is that which is No Thing. A thing is that which 'exists' in the Universe either physically or mentally. No Thing would mean, that which does not exist physically or mentally. Anything that doesn't exist physically or mentally for us is actually nothing. Nothing cannot be perceived or experienced by the five senses or the mind because it is neither physical nor mental."

"Nothing is therefore non-existent in the Universe AND if it were existing then it certainly isn't that which we can experience physically or mentally. We need not fear anything that isn't physical or mental. Think about it, all our fears and problems in life are either physical or mental."

"Only a thing can harm or damage another thing. Only a thing can do something to your body or mind. 'Nothing' is completely harmless and not worth pondering over or bothering about. Just as the dictionary says, 'nothing' is insignificant, worthless, without substance and of no importance. Who has ever bothered about nothing? Who has sleepless nights because of nothing? 'Nothing' is absolutely useless. It cannot be 'used' for anything."

"What can we use nothing for? It cannot be used for anything; we cannot 'do' anything to it. We cannot do anything 'with' it. It cannot do anything to us. It cannot do anything to anybody or anything else. Truly, what good can nothing be for us? As a person, nothing is worthless and not worth pursuing or wasting our time and effort on."

"Great! Do you get the same feeling with all the other words we equated with nothing? What good is Pure Existence, Pure Consciousness, Pure Bliss, Brahman, Nirvana, Tao, Self or God? They're no good to a 'person' for the same reasons. We can't use any of them for anything. We can't do anything 'to' them. We can't do anything 'with' them. They don't seem to be doing anything at all."

"This is straight talk. For those who may be offended about putting God in the same category, let me clarify that God's existence cannot be proven and therefore we cannot blame or praise God for anything and everything going on in the Universe (This is nothing against God as you will find out)."

"'Nothing' is as true as Brahman, Nirvana, Tao, Pure Existence, Pure Consciousness, Pure Bliss, God, Absolute Truth and Absolute Reality. They all don't exist physically or mentally. They cannot be perceived by our five senses and/or our mind. They are all BEYOND the perception or experience of any living being. They are all BEYOND a person's reach or grasp."

"None of them exist in the Universe. If there is one entity that you can be one thousand percent sure of that exists in this Universe, it has to be YOU! To name anything or anybody else in your place YOU would still have to exist before it or them. Everything in the Universe is a 'thing' to you. You may also feel that you are one of the 'things' in the Universe. And that would be correct when referring to your person (body mind complex)."

"You (as a person) are definitely one of the things existing in the Universe BUT let me ask you this. Do you really feel (not think) that you are a thing or an object in the Universe? No! No person in the world feels that they are a thing or an object. Deep within every person, they feel they are the Subject to everything else in the Universe."

"Every person has an internal first hand Subjective view of their life. You experience your life as the Subject experiencing objects. You never feel that you are a thing experiencing other things. You always feel within that you are not a thing but a being that is conscious, aware and alive."

"But when it comes to say something about yourself, you will say 'things' about your body and mind and claim that that is what or who you are. For example, I am John, forty years old and live in England. John, forty years old and England refer to the person (body mind complex)."

"What you 'think' or 'know' yourself to be is known as your 'ego'. Your ego claims 'I am this or that, here or there, then or when, who or what.' Anything you add AFTER the words 'I Am' refers to your body or mind (the person). The ego is in the mind and our lives are experienced in the mind hence we feel that we ARE the mind. The mind is only a bundle of thoughts BUT 'I AM' is not a thought, the words that follow 'I Am' are thoughts."

"The 'I Am' in you is not a thought, it is the feeling or the knowing that you are NOT a thing, NOT an object in the Universe BUT the Subject to everything else in the Universe. The 'I Am' in you is the ONE thing that is not a thought but a fact for you. Everything in the Universe may or may not exist BUT 'I Am' is not open to doubt."

"What is this 'I Am' in every living being? It is not a thought; it is not anything physical or mental, it is not a thing, it is no thing, it is NOTHING! Your 'I Am' is NOTHING. Your 'I Am' is exactly the same as Brahman, God, Pure Existence, Pure Consciousness etc. as we have seen earlier."

"Let's go through the power of nothing next and then we'll inquire into your 'I Am' and see whether they tally, whether they're the same entity, whether they exist etc." said Swamiji, as he reached out to grab his glass for a sip of water.

Richard had noted down some strong statements hoping Swamiji would finally put it all together in the end. There was too much of *nothing* going on in his head.

Nothing Is That
Which Is
Not A Thing,
No Thing,
Non-Existent!

You May Know
What Nothing
Means
BUT
You CANNOT Know
What Nothing
IS!

You Cannot See, Hear, Smell, Taste Or Touch Nothing!

You Cannot Think, Imagine, Remember Dream Or Understand Nothing!

Nothing Does Not Exist Physically Or Mentally!

NOTHING IS:
Harmless,
Useless,
Worthless,
Insignificant,
Without Substance,
Of No Importance
In The Universe!

The Same Goes For:
The Absolute Truth,
Brahman & God!

> Nothing, Brahman, Absolute Truth & God Don't Exist In The Universe Like Every 'Thing' Else Does!
>
> They Are BEYOND A Person's Experience Or Perception!

*Your 'I AM'
Is Not A Thing!*

*Your 'I AM'
Is NOTHING!*

**ABSOLUTE TRUTH,
BRAHMAN,
TRUE SELF,
GOD & 'I AM'
=
NOTHING!**

The Power Of Nothing

THE POWER OF NOTHING

Swamiji had a few sips of water; the night was a little warmer than the previous one but still cold enough to wear warm clothes. Swamiji knew very well what he was doing with his talk. He knew that most of the people wouldn't really be interested in knowing *nothing* and maybe the talks till now would have bored some of them but it was important to lay down the foundation of what he wanted to convey before giving them what they were actually seeking. He also knew that these were learned people who had read philosophy and spiritual books.

Words such as *Brahman, Nirvana, Freedom, Liberation, Pure Consciousness, Pure Existence, Pure Bliss, Sat-Chit-Ananda, God, Supreme Being, Purusha, Cosmic Self, True Self, Pure Awareness, Atman* and many more were not new to any of these special invitees from Europe. In fact they could teach others about these terms.

He also knew that any new word or term given to a seeker would send him or her rushing to attain that 'thing'. Most of them knew about *Brahman* and the Upanishads but had still not realized the teachings. Most of them were still *searching* for God or their True Self.

Everyone knows what nothing is; yet no one knows what it is. The word 'nothing' was the perfect replacement for all the complicated words such as *Brahman, Absolute Reality, Pure Existence or Pure Consciousness.*

Another reason for using the word *nothing* was *non-duality. Nothing* is non-dual, one without a second. There are no two types of nothings. There is only ONE *nothing* AND it is non-dual. A perfect match with the definition of *God* and *Brahman* and all the other terms and words. Swamiji continued his talk.

"Let's look at the Power of Nothing now. Remember we equated 'Nothing' with Brahman, Nirvana, Freedom, Liberation, Non-duality, Pure Existence, Pure Consciousness, Pure Bliss, God, The Supreme Being, The Absolute Truth and The Absolute Reality. The qualities of all of them are ABSOLUTELY the same. If Brahman is non-dual, then so is God or the Absolute Reality. If Pure Consciousness is everywhere, every time and in everything then so is the Supreme Being and so on."

"We also saw that 'nothing' is worthless for anyone or anything in the Universe. I'll reveal some of the powers of nothing. Nothing is immortal. Nothing is formless. Nothing is infinite. Nothing is non-dual (One without a second). Nothing is unborn and can never die."

"Nothing transcends all pain, sorrow and suffering. Nothing is everywhere, every time and everything. Nothing is completely fearless. Nothing fulfills ALL worldly desires in an instant. Nothing is ONE with everything and everybody in the Universe. Nothing is Divinity itself. Nothing is true freedom and liberation. Nothing reveals everything to be an illusion or appearance of itself."

"You may say, 'well good for nothing, what is it to me?' Nothing is your 'I Am'. Nothing is your true identity. Nothing is YOU! You are all the things I just mentioned. Yes you are immortal, infinite, formless, non-dual, untouched by pain and suffering, one with the Universe and divinity itself.

"He who knows nothing knows everything. He who achieves nothing achieves everything. He who does nothing does everything. He who knows nothing has known what is to be known in life. He who achieved nothing has achieved what is to be achieved in life. He who knows nothing has done what is to be done in life. He who knows nothing becomes nothing. He who is nothing is the truth or reality of everything."

"This 'knowing' of Nothing/Brahman/God is neither a physical experience nor a mental experience. Everything we know is known in our mind. Nothing/Brahman/God cannot be known by the mind. The 'knowing' of Nothing/Brahman/God is a DIRECT knowing, direct experience or direct perception. There is no gap or distance, physically or mentally between what is known and you. You ARE what you know, you ARE what you experience and you ARE what you perceive. You know without the mind that you ARE Nothing/Brahman/God."

"This is the Power of Nothing and YOU. ARE. NOTHING! We'll take a tea break and when we come back, we'll inquire into your 'I Am' and see first hand if YOU actually ARE everything that I've just said. Not intellectually, not logically, not through a physical experience, not through a mental experience BUT a DIRECT experience of YOU/NOTHING/BRAHMAN/GOD," said Swamiji as he took off his microphone and came down the stage to join the rest for some hot *chai* and snacks.

THE POWER OF NOTHING:

Nothing Is IMMORTAL!
Nothing Is FORMLESS!
Nothing Is NON-DUAL!
Nothing Is UNBORN!
Nothing Transcends Pain & Suffering!

Nothing Is Everywhere, Every Time & Everything!
Nothing Is FEARLESS!
Nothing Fulfils All Worldly Desires In An Instant!
Nothing Is YOU!

The Power Of Nothing

I AM NOTHING

After the tea break everyone went back to his or her seats and Swamiji took his position on the stage, put on his microphone and began his talk. This was going to be interesting. Everything that Swamiji had claimed as nothing was to be directly experienced by the audience as promised by Swamiji.

Richard was so excited because this would finally be something that they were going to experience rather than think and learn. He was seated right at the front row at the edge of his seat with his eyes fixed on Swamiji.

"Right, like I said before going for the break, when we come back we will inquire into your 'I Am' and see if it tallies with nothing and all the other big words such as Brahman, Nirvana, Pure Existence etc."

"I would like a volunteer to work with while the rest of you can follow the same instructions," said Swamiji. Richard was the first to put up his hand and Swamiji called upon him to come on stage. Richard couldn't believe his luck and was almost in tears.

Once on stage, Richard sat opposite Swamiji. He could feel love and warmth radiating from Swamiji. Time seemed to slow down and Richard was almost completely at peace. His mind had calmed down.

"Welcome. What is your name?" asked Swamiji with a smile. *"Richard. I'm from London. Thank you so much for having me here,"* replied Richard, excited and nervous at the same time. *"Welcome Richard. I'm going to work with you to go past your body and mind, find your 'I Am' and then we'll inquire as to whether it is what all the enlightened masters and scriptures are talking about."*

"Everybody else please follow along and try to experience it for yourself as well. We'll have a questions and answers session after this, in case anyone needs more clarity on anything we have discussed so far."

"Richard I welcome you on stage. I suppose you presently identify yourself with your body and mind. Is that right?" asked Swamiji. *"Yes Swamiji,"* replied Richard. *"You are a person that has a tangible or physical body and an intangible or subtle mind."*

"I would like you to empty your mind of all thoughts. Drop all the thoughts for the next few minutes. Drop all thoughts about your past, present and/or your future. Drop all your life experiences since childhood. Drop the life drama that plays in your mind. Have a completely BLANK mind."

"No mental voice chattering and no mental images flashing. Not even the thought of 'what next?' Once you have a completely blank mind and absolutely no thoughts, let me know. And everyone else please follow the same instructions," said Swamiji looking at the rest.

Richard took a couple of minutes and settled down. He mentally stopped thinking, until he was only aware of his breath inhaling and exhaling. *"Yes Swamiji. My mind is empty. My mind is blank. There is nothing,"* said Richard.

"Great! You have a blank mind. There is nothing at all. Now I would like you to drop the awareness of your body and the surroundings. Simply don't pay any attention to any 'thing' including your body or anything around us. Now there should be absolutely nothing. Is that right?" asked Swamiji, looking at Richard.

"Yes Swamiji, there's nothing," replied Richard. He looked like he was staring mid air, not looking or seeing anything. *"There is nothing right now but are you still there?"* asked Swamiji. *"Yes Swamiji, I am still there,"* replied Richard.

"There is nothing and you. Observe and pay attention to this nothingness. You'll find that it is not a thing but it still IS. It has some sort of issness or existence to it. It IS, you can't tell what or who it is but you can't deny that it IS," said Swamiji.

Immediately Richard looked like he was taken by surprise. His eyes lit up and eyebrows raised and a smile came upon his face, *"Yes Swamiji, the nothingness is. It just is, you're right; it isn't a thing BUT IT IS. It has some sort of issness to it,"* replied Richard still staring mid air but with a smile like he had discovered something miraculous.

"That's a good way of putting it, I'll use the words nothingness or issness to refer to it. Let's inquire into what this nothingness is. Let me ask you some questions and answer them honestly from what you are directly experiencing and not from your mind."

"Where is this nothingness?" asked Swamiji. Richard spoke after a few seconds, *"It is everywhere,"* *"Does it have a beginning, a middle or an ending?"* asked Swamiji, and Richard again spoke after a few seconds, *"No Swamiji, it has no beginning, no middle or ending."* *"Does this nothingness have a shape, a size or any form?"* asked Swamiji, and this time Richard was quick to reply, *"No it doesn't have any shape, size or form."*

"Can you see it with your eyes, smell it with your nose, hear it with your ears, taste it with your tongue of touch it with your skin?" asked Swamiji. *"No I can't,"* replied Richard.

"Did this nothingness just come up now that we started inquiring?" asked Swamiji. *"No,"* came the reply. *"Where has it been all this while?"* asked Swamiji. *"It's always been there,"* replied Richard.

"Was this nothingness ever born?" asked Swamiji. *"No, it was never born,"* came the reply. *"Can it ever die?"* probed Swamiji. *"No it cannot die,"* came the reply.

"Can it ever go away?" asked Swamiji. *"No it can't,"* replied Richard. *"Can you get rid of it if you wanted?"* asked Swamiji. *"No I can't,"* came the reply.

"Can this nothingness ever be affected by disease or old age?" asked Swamiji. *"No,"* came the instant reply.

"Can it be affected by pain and suffering?" asked Swamiji. *"No,"* replied Richard.

"Is there anything that exists outside this nothingness?" continued Swamiji. *"No,"* came the reply. By now Richard understood that anything that Swamiji said about this nothingness would be wrong.

"Does this nothingness need to become rich and famous?" asked Swamiji, and Richard burst out laughing. *"No Swamiji, it doesn't need to become rich or famous,"* he replied.

"Does it need to become spiritually enlightened?" asked Swamiji, like he had memorized these questions. *"No it doesn't,"* replied Richard.

"Can you do anything 'with' or 'to' this nothingness?" continued Swamiji. *"No,"* came the prompt reply.

"When your body dies, will this nothingness still be there?" asked Swamiji. *"Yes,"* came the reply.

"How far away from you is this nothingness?" asked Swamiji. *"It's not far at all,"* replied Richard. *"Is there any distance or even a slight gap between you and this nothingness?"* continued Swamiji. *"No Swamiji, there's no gap at all,"* replied Richard, looking a little serious now.

"If there is no distance between you and this nothingness, then it must be you. Is this nothingness you?" asked Swamiji. Richard took a few seconds before confirming, *"Yes Swamiji, it is me."*

"If this nothingness is you, then all the answers given prior to this were about you. You were never born, you are unaffected by pain and suffering, you are everywhere, every time and everything, you cannot be affected by old age and disease, you don't need to become rich and famous, you can never die etc." said Swamiji.

"Let's check if this nothingness is what the scriptures talk about. Brahman is pure existence and pure consciousness infinite. If this nothingness doesn't have a beginning, middle or an ending, if this nothingness has no shape, size or form, then it must be infinite and formless. Is it infinite and formless?" asked Swamiji. *"Yes it is,"* replied Richard.

"Is this nothingness a thing?" asked Swamiji. *"No,"* came the reply. *"Does this nothingness exist in any way or form?"* asked Swamiji. *"No, it is Existence itself. It exists without a thing. It is existence without a thing,"* replied Richard.

"Is this nothingness conscious of any thing?" asked Swamiji. *"No, it's only conscious of itself. It is not conscious of any thing, it is Consciousness itself,"* replied Richard. *"So this nothingness is the same as the Self or Brahman of the Upanishads,"* said Swamiji.

"Is this nothingness blissful?" asked Swamiji. *"No Swamiji, it is bliss itself,"* replied Richard.

"Is this nothingness peaceful?" asked Swamiji. *"No, it is peace itself,"* came the reply.

"Is it some kind of Being?" asked Swamiji. *"No, it is Being itself. It is the ONLY Being,"* replied Richard.

"Is this nothingness God?" asked Swamiji. Richard took a minute to answer this. *"No Swamiji, it is NOT God,"* replied Richard. Swamiji looked at him with a smile and asked, *"Is it one with God?" "Yes Swamiji, it is one with God. It is one with me and one with God. It is not God but it is not apart from God,"* replied Richard. Swamiji seemed very pleased with Richard's answers.

"I think this will be enough," said Swamiji. He had a smile on his face. Richard seemed to be stunned, like he had been in the presence of the divine. *"Did any of you have the same direct experience?"* asked Swamiji looking at the others. About twenty out of thirty hands went up. Some people were in tears of joy while a few others were absolutely silent and in a trance like state.

"I'll take some questions now. These two nights, like I said earlier will sow a seed, which if watered regularly will sprout and grow into a huge tree. Our staff members will come around with a microphone. Please ask your question into the microphone so that everyone can hear it," said Swamiji.

QUESTIONS & ANSWERS

Two monks went around with cordless microphones handing them to whoever put up their hand. Swamiji spent the next forty minutes answering all the questions until sunrise. This was the last night for everyone and everyone wanted to make sure they had clarity about what Swamiji had shared.

The following are only six of the questions that were put forward by those present and the answers that Swamiji gave as well.

Question 1:

Swamiji, you mentioned that everything known by mankind in the Universe is only 'relatively' true and that God is the only 'absolute' truth. You also explained that God and the Absolute Truth is nothing that we can perceive with our senses and mind. Can you please give me an example because it seems like you're saying that everything is relatively true compared to nothing. How are we to understand this?

Swamiji:

Let's take up the dream example for this. When you are dreaming, you experience a whole dream universe. For as long as you are dreaming, everything in the dream world seems absolutely real. The people, places, time, your body and mind seem very real to you. But in the instant that you wake up, you realize that it was just a dream.

You were in the dream for a fact. You also experienced everything in the dream for a fact. But when you woke up, everything in the dream was nullified as not real. Everything that happened in the dream did NOT REALLY happen. It's true that you experienced the dream and it's also true that nothing really happened.

The dream is relatively true when compared to your waking state. In the same way when you realize the absolute truth, this waking state that seems to be so real will be nullified as NOT real. This waking state (your life) will be realized to be a dream. It will be as real as your dream was. Everything in the dream state is nothing of the waking state. Everything in the dream was true until you woke you, when you woke up "NOTHING" WAS TRUE! When you wake up from a dream, the dream ends BUT when you wake up to God or your True Self the identification with the person (body and mind) ends!

Question 2:

Swamiji, you said that God is nothing, Brahman is nothing, the Absolute Truth is nothing and even the 'I am' is nothing. Does it mean that they don't exist or that they're not there?

Swamiji:

Yes I did say that. God, Brahman, Absolute Truth, Self, I Am etc. is nothing. Everything is something. Everybody is somebody. God IS nothing. Please pay attention to the IS. It means that God IS. Period. God is NOT this or that. Any word you put after the IS, is NOT what God is. Any word you put AFTER the word IS, is NOT what Brahman is, is not what the Absolute Truth is, is not what the true Self is and is not what I Am is.

Every other word in the English vocabulary and dictionary refers to a thing, either physical or mental. The ONLY word in the English vocabulary that refers to that which is NOT A THING is nothing. God or Brahman IS means that whatever IS, is God or Brahman. God/Brahman/Self alone IS, everyTHING else is NOT.

I Am IS NOT whatever word you put AFTER I Am. For example if I say, I am a doctor. The 'I Am' is NOT a doctor. 'Doctor' is the work or profession of the person (body mind complex). Only because someone identifies himself as the person, he says 'I am a doctor.' The 'I Am' still remains as it is, even if the 'doctor' tag is removed. The 'I Am' is untouched by any word that supersedes it. The 'I Am' is NOT any word you put AFTER it. The 'I Am' IS what it is. Any word trying to describe it is NOT IT.

So God is nothing does not mean that God is not, it means that God IS not this or that. God IS. If God IS then everything else IS NOT. The Dreamer IS, everything in the dream IS NOT. The Dreamer is nothing in the dream. In reality the Dreamer alone IS. The dream is NOT. God/Brahman alone IS, the Universe is NOT. The Dreamer is NOTHING in the dream. God is NOTHING in the Universe. The dream is nothing BUT the Dreamer. The Universe is nothing BUT God.

It may sound paradoxical because one IS and the other APPEARS to be. For example, if you saw Richard playing the role of a king in a play. Richard will APPEAR as the king on stage BUT in reality he is Richard. In the same way, the Universe APPEARS as things, in REALITY the Universe IS God. The king is not Richard; the REALITY of the king is Richard.

Question 3:
Swamiji, are you sure that the word 'nothing' can replace all the other words that have been used to point to the Absolute Reality? Can the word 'nothing' be used to replace all those other words? If so, please explain.

Swamiji:
ABSOLUTELY! The words such as Brahman, infinity, formless, non-duality, absolute truth/reality etc. all point to that which is NOT A THING, to that which cannot be grasped by the senses, the mind or the intellect. For example, Brahman cannot be perceived by the five senses, so let's imagine we shut down all our senses. If Brahman cannot be seen it is nothing to the eyes. If Brahman cannot be heard it is noting to the ears. And if Brahman cannot be tasted, smelled or touched, it is nothing to the tongue, nose and skin.

So, Brahman is that when the eyes see nothing, the ears hear nothing, the nose smells nothing, the tongue tastes nothing and the skin touches nothing. We can easily put ourselves in that state for sometime. If you put on a blindfold, you will see nothing. If you wear earplugs, you will hear nothing, if you wash and clean your tongue, you will taste nothing, if you will clear the air in your room, you will smell nothing and if you do not move your body about, you will touch nothing.

In this state when you are sensing NOTHING from outside, the only thing going on will be the thoughts in your mind. Brahman cannot be known by the mind. Your mind is only a bundle of thoughts and if you stop your thoughts for a few seconds or minutes then you have actually put yourself in the state of nothingness. There is nothing to experience physically or mentally. A more powerful way of putting it is, 'directly experiencing the NOTHINGNESS without your body and mind'.

Experiencing Brahman or the Nothingness is exactly the same direct experience. Realizing your true identity as Brahman, or realizing your true identity as nothing, is absolutely the same. Nothing is everything that Brahman is. Brahman is non-dual, one without a second. So is nothing. There is only ONE nothing in the Universe.

You can safely replace any of the words pointing to the absolute reality with the word nothing. The only reason for using this word (nothing) is because we have already been using it from childhood. We know what it means BUT we don't know what it IS.

If I told you, 'You are Brahman, realize it,' your mind immediately wants to know what Brahman means and how it can be realized. You learn that Brahman is Pure Existence Pure Consciousness Infinite and you try to realize yourself as Pure Existence or Pure Consciousness making it a complex search for something that is not a thing.

BUT if I told you, 'You are Nothing, realize it,' your mind immediately stops because it knows what nothing means but it has never paid any attention to it. Your mind has no problem knowing what nothing means as long as you don't try to inquire deeper into it. Think about it, whenever you sit to meditate and try to think of NOTHING, the mind goes into overdrive with thoughts. The mind will never let you REALIZE NOTHING, it has no problem with you visiting nothing now and then BUT REALIZING NOTHING as your own true Self is equivalent to death of the mind (ego). And the mind is designed to fight and survive for as long as it can.

Brahman is not similar or like nothing, it IS Nothing! You are Brahman but you don't know Brahman. In the same way you are nothing (not a thing) but you don't know nothing.

One more point I'd like to clear here is that this nothingness that you directly experienced here as your true Self is NOT God but ONE with you and ONE with God.

Using the popular Wave and Ocean example, Water is ONE with the Wave AND the Ocean. The wave is NOT the Ocean; it is a part of the Ocean. The Ocean is the whole and the wave is a part BUT both are ONE with Water. In the same way, your true identity as the Self or Nothingness is ONE with the identity of God BUT God is the whole infinite Universe and you are a part of the Universe or God. The Wave cannot be the Ocean. You cannot be God. The Wave AS Water is ONE with the Ocean. You AS the Nothingness are ONE with God/Universe.

Question 4:
Swamiji, what happens when you realize Brahman or Nothing as you're saying?

Swamiji:
When you realize Brahman/Nothing, you become Brahman/Nothing. You realize that you always were and are not a thing. You realize that you are what IS. You also realize that everything in the Universe is NOT what your mind 'calls' it or 'thinks' it to be. Every 'thing' in the Universe IS WHAT IT IS, IT JUST IS. The Universe IS what it IS, it is NOT what your mind 'thinks' it is. You realize your Self as the entire Universe, which IS what it IS, not what your mind 'thinks' it is. What your mind thinks is a thought, NOT IT!

Question 5:
Swamiji, I did the exercise as you were instructing us to do and I did experience the nothingness and yes I did confirm that the nothingness is my true identity or I. I also confirmed that the nothingness has always been there and that it can never go away or die. It will always be there. Does this mean that I am spiritually enlightened now?

Swamiji:
Good try my child, but not so fast. There is a process that involves destruction of your present identity (ego) and emergence of your true identity (Brahman/Nothingness). When that occurs and

your 'I' shifts from the person to the nothingness, then you may say that the person you are is spiritually enlightened. Brahman/Nothingness doesn't need enlightenment/freedom/liberation etc. The 'person' needs freedom and enlightenment. The 'person' doesn't attain freedom or liberation. YOU attain freedom FROM the person. YOU are liberated FROM the person.

The person may be called enlightened simply because enlightenment happens in the intellect (mind) and the intellect is part of the person. The 'person' may be called enlightened but not 'you' as Brahman/Nothingness.

How to destroy the ego into the nothingness? First make sure your mind is fully convinced about this nothingness intellectually. Absolute conviction by the mind is required that this is true. The slightest doubt or fear will hold you back. So get all your doubts cleared and have complete clarity about this nothingness.

Next, back your knowledge with all your faith and belief. This is not blind faith and belief; it is faith and belief in what you have understood to be true. Since you have had a taste or glimpse of the nothingness, now your only effort is to water this seed regularly for as long as you can. Visit this nothingness and abide in it AS IT. Soak yourself in this nothingness as often as you can with the faith and belief that it is the truth and/or your true Self.

Now comes the most essential part, Grace of God/Guru/Self. When God/Guru/Self sees that you (the person) are sincere and genuine in your quest with no 'personal' desires including that of liberation or freedom. You are doing it because it is what you know and believe to be the absolute truth, then by the Grace of God/Guru/Self your (the person's) ego will be swallowed up, dissolved, destroyed and merged with the nothingness never to return again. This ego destruction/dissolution will happen in an instant if the mind is ready. This is an experience that your mind will never forget.

Or the ego may slowly be broken down over a period of time and the last bit of it swallowed up in a similar experience that your mind will never forget. It may also occur slowly over period of time and completely dissolve without any dramatic experience happening in the end. It will depend on the readiness of the mind and your dedication and sincerity. That's why I said to water this seed (nothingness) regularly.

Question 6:
What should we do when abiding as the nothingness?

Swamiji:
*Remember these three things to get you in the state of nothingness immediately. **Don't move. Don't speak. Don't think.** Keep your body still, don't speak anything verbally and don't think anything. Thoughts will bubble up in your mind whether you like it or not. Thinking only happens when you pay attention to a thought and that leads to other thoughts. So simply don't pay attention to any thoughts that bubble up and eventually they will fizzle out.*

When you don't move, speak or think, you will be faced with nothing (blank mind). Observe and inquire into this nothingness with as many questions as you can into what it is. You will find it is everything that the spiritual scriptures talk about and most importantly that it is YOU. YOU ARE NOTHING THAT IS IMMORTAL AND PURE BLISS! What thing in the Universe can be more powerful than NO THING? YOU. ARE. THAT. YOU. ARE. NOTHING!

The above were just six of the many questions that were put forward to Swamiji. The sun was up, breakfast was served and everyone relished the hot *chai* and *samosas*. Richard met with everyone and left for his room. He had a flight from Amritsar back to the UK later in the day. As he left the lawn, the monks were handing out a booklet of instructions titled *"The Power Of Nothing"* to everyone that had the instructions of inquiry into nothingness printed on it.

Richard hurried towards his room and quickly packed his suitcase. Many others had flights back home on the same day, while others were checking out from the ashram to go explore other cities in India.

Richard called for a taxi to take him to the airport. As he waited at the reception area for the taxi he pulled out the book he was reading on the way here and happened to open it on exactly the same page where he was scratching his head trying to understand the words as follows:

"He who knows nothing and knows that it cannot be known truly knows. He who does nothing and knows that it cannot do anything truly does. He who speaks nothing and knows that it cannot be spoken truly speaks. He who is nothing and knows that he is not a thing truly is."

"Let me see if I understand this now," thought Richard to himself. He tried to comprehend it from the nothingness point of view that he had experienced with Swamiji on stage.

He who knows nothing and knows that it cannot be known truly knows.
I know that the Nothing-ness known through *direct experience* cannot be known by the mind.

He who does nothing and knows that it cannot do anything truly does.
The Nothing-ness that I am *does nothing* and *cannot do anything* and yet I (the person) continue to do.

He who speaks nothing and knows that it cannot be speak truly speaks.
The Nothing-ness that I am *doesn't speak* and *cannot speak* and yet I (the person) continue to speak.

He who is nothing and knows that he is not a thing truly is.
The Nothing-ness that I am knows that 'I Am' is not a thing.

Richard smiled to himself as he thought through all the statements. *"Who can make such statements except he who knows both the relative and the absolute reality,"* said Richard, shaking his head in disbelief as he sat in the taxi that would take him to the airport just in time for his flight to the UK.

"Everything is at the level of the mind and the Universe. 'Nothing' is at the level of the Absolute Truth/Reality. 'Nothing' transcends everything of the Universe/Mind. I guess I have to soak and marinate myself IN the nothingness AS the nothingness," were his last thoughts before having his dinner and falling asleep on the flight.

EXTRA NOTES

Since I began writing about spirituality and non-duality, THIS is the book that I wanted to write. It tidies up and organizes the madness known as the Universe, then proceeds to tidy up and organize the entity known as the Absolute Truth so one can clearly be pointed to something he or she knows but has never paid attention to.

It's impossible to know everything in the Universe but if you understand what a *thing* is then you would know *something, that thing, this thing and everything.* You would know everything in the Universe.

It's impossible to understand what in the Universe all the spiritual scriptures are pointing to, but once you understand that everything in the Universe is some kind of *thing* AND that the Sages, Saints and Spiritual Scriptures all point to *THAT* which cannot be perceived or experienced by the body or mind (which is how everything in the Universe is experienced or perceived), then you understand that what they're pointing to is *not a thing.* It is NOTHING!

Brahman/Existence/Consciousness/God is neither a thing nor a body. It IS *nothing or nobody.* Now you don't need to understand what pure existence is because *nothing* is pure existence, *nothing* is pure consciousness, *nothing* is Brahman, *nothing* is pure bliss, *nothing* is love itself, peace itself, stillness itself, silence itself etc.

I really hope this book would have cleared a lot of clutter in your quest to realize the Absolute Divine Truth that YOU ARE. You need not try to understand and realize huge words and difficult terms. You have always known what nothing meant; now EXPOSE yourself to nothing, INQUIRE into the nothingness and LOSE yourself into the nothingness.

As long as you are *something* or *somebody* in the Universe, the mind is happy. The mind will resist when you try to realize yourself as *nothing* or *nobody*. All this realization is at the *level* of the mind. In one sentence, *'Inquire what is aware of the nothingness in a blank mind.'*

The following are some nuggets that I would've liked to put in the story but they would have disrupted the flow of thoughts going from the known to the unknown so I will mention them here in the form of little nuggets in no particular order. They're all relevant to the information in this book. You never know which one is going to put all your non-dual knowledge together so you get it beyond a doubt.

1. *"A 'thing' is that which has a particular name, form and use. It is that which is limited in time, space and object identity. It is that which you are aware of or conscious of. It is an object to 'you', the Subject. This includes the physical Universe externally and your thoughts internally. Every 'thing' including your body, mind and thoughts is a 'thing' to you, the Subject of all of them. Mentally take the 'thing' out of every 'thing' (everything) and see what remains. Mentally take the 'body' out of every 'body' (everybody) and see what remains."*

__2.__ "After knowing what 'nothing' is now, if someone tells you that there's nothing like Brahman, Pure Consciousness, Pure Existence, Absolute Truth, Absolute Reality, Pure Awareness or God, let them know they are ABSOLUTELY right but encourage them to find out what nothing IS because it IS nothing."

__3.__ "Pure Consciousness/Brahman is sometimes described as the 'Witness' or "Witness Consciousness". The Nothing-ness that you (hopefully) experienced is absolutely that. The Nothing-ness that YOU are IS a 'Witness' to everything going on in your life (the person). The Nothing-ness cannot and does not 'do' anything. It simply is there as a 'Witness'."

__4.__ "Make sure once you are convinced of this nothingness and have all your doubts cleared, then plunge into this Nothing-ness with the utmost faith and belief in what you are intellectually convinced about beyond doubt. Half hearted effort will not do."

5. *"Thousands of words have been written and uttered by Great Saints, Sages and Avatars yet none of them can confirm that 'THIS' is the Absolute Truth. Words can only be about physical or mental 'things' and we have already seen that the Absolute Truth is Not A Thing. Hence anyTHING and everyTHING said and written about the Absolute Truth cannot BE the Absolute Truth. The Absolute Truth Is Not A Thing. It Is NOTHING! In fact, you can give it whatever name you want as long it points to the Nothing-ness mentally. Use any word that works best for you. Remember the Absolute is Nameless, so any word used by you should only point you to that Nothing-ness."*

6. *"The Grace of God/Guru/Self shines forth upon the individual person when he or she wholeheartedly WANTS absolutely nothing. Who wants to do that? To want and desire nothing and become nothing SHOULD and CAN ONLY be internally in the MIND and NOT externally. You can be a king and yet be attached to nothing mentally. You may be a 'somebody' externally to the world and yet are a 'nobody' internally in your mind. Mentally get rid of every thing that you are attached to until you are attached to NOTHING! Mentally get rid of all your ideas, concepts and notions about yourself until you are NOTHING! On the outside in the physical world continue to do what needs to be done, internally do not be attached to who is doing and what is being done!*

7. *"Do everyTHING until all the doing is done. Say everyTHING until all the saying is said. Think all the thoughts until all the thinking is thought. THEN bring to rest all three (body, tongue and mind) and ABIDE AS the Nothing-ness that is 'feeling' rested. All three should be brought to rest at the same time and not one by one. Just be!*

8. *The Vedantic method of Neti-Neti results in NOTHING! 'Neti-Neti' is the method that literally means 'Not this - Not this'. It simply means that anyTHING that the mind can say 'this' to is NOT the Absolute Truth/Reality. Not this, not this, until you reach the point where your mind should dismiss any thought as NOT the Absolute Reality. Literally saying that the Absolute Truth is NOTHING! It is THAT which is BEFORE any thought.*

9. *A 'thing' is only a 'thought' in your mind. Mentally detach yourself from every thought. Don't try to get rid of it BUT MENTALLY 'DETACH' YOU from every thought until the 'YOU' that you know directly is absolutely NOTHING & NOBODY!*

10. *Nothing is Impossible! This saying is absolutely true. It is a motivational saying which means that, 'anyTHING and everyTHING IS POSSIBLE! Anything and everything is possible for the person at the body and mind level (relative truth/reality). NOTHING IS IMPOSSIBLE (for the body or mind). The Nothing-ness is impossible at the body and mind level (relative truth/reality). Nothing is impossible (in the relative state). Nothing is possible (in the absolute state).*

11. *"We have always understood 'nothing' from the negative perspective i.e. not a thing, not this or that, non-existent BUT I would like you to look at it from the positive perspective i.e. the fact that it IS. It may not be a 'who' or a 'what' but it IS. This Issness should replace the idea of dismissing nothing as that which isn't because it IS."*

12. *I'll share a few ways of 'sensing' a strong undeniable 'direct' experience of the Self instantly, so you know what it 'feels' like. Try them and I sincerely hope they work for you.*

The First One: *Sit comfortably and when you're ready, close your hands into fists, curl your toes inwards and tightly clench your entire body including your arms, legs, abdomen and eyes closed. Hold your breath for 2-3 seconds with the clenched body. In these 2-3 seconds notice without a thought in the mind that there is an "awareness" of the darkness behind your closed eyes and around the body. This "Awareness" is what the*

Nothing-ness 'feels' like. Once you let go, try to recall that 'feeling' of when the body was stiff and the mind was frozen in those 2-3 seconds. That 'feeling' is what is Pure Awareness/Pure Consciousness/Pure Existence/Nothingness etc. This clenching is only to give you the 'feeling' of awareness and NOT to keep clenching all the time.

The Second One: *I would like you to mentally prepare yourself to say the words 'I Am'. Once you have mentally prepared to say the words, go ahead and say them EXCEPT that at the very last millisecond when the tongue and the mind are about to utter the words, close your lips and stop. Immediately notice an awareness around and inside the head. It will last for 1-2 seconds only; you have to notice it within that time. That Awareness is what you should be looking for.*

The Third One: *While seated comfortably, imagine that someone in front of you has a balloon that he will burst close to your face. You'll realize that your body is preparing for that loud bang by being still and the mind stopping for the few seconds before the bang. Notice the 'stillness feeling' of the body and mind before the balloon bursts. That 'feeling' is what you should be looking for. That is Pure Awareness, Pure Consciousness, Stillness or Nothingness etc.*

Thank you for reading. I felt it is important to add all these points. I sincerely and genuinely hope you realize the Absolute Truth in this lifetime itself. In the following pages we have a 'Step-by-Step Summary Booklet' of the teachings as noted by Richard on his notepad followed by the 'Power Of Nothing Instructions Booklet' that was handed out to everyone at the end of the two-nights satsang. Stay blessed....

NOTHING MORE NEED BE SAID, DONE OR THOUGHT.

ABIDE AS NOTHING IN THE NOTHING-NESS!!!

A STEP BY STEP SUMMARY OF THE TEACHINGS!

"RELATIVE" TRUTH
IS:
The Universe,
The self,
The Finite,
The Known,
A Thing,
EVERYTHING!

"RELATIVE" TRUTH
IS NOT:
God,
The SELF,
The Infinite,
The Unknown,
Not A Thing,
NOTHING!

> **"ABSOLUTE" TRUTH IS:**
> God,
> The SELF,
> The Infinite,
> The Unknown,
> Not A Thing,
> NOTHING!
>
> **"ABSOLUTE" TRUTH IS NOT:**
> The Universe,
> The self,
> The Finite,
> The Known,
> A Thing,
> EVERYTHING!

YOU ARE BOTH THE "RELATIVE" TRUTH **AND** THE "ABSOLUTE" TRUTH!

YOUR "I AM" IS THE "ABSOLUTE" TRUTH **AND** EVERYTHING **AFTER** YOUR "I AM" IS THE "RELATIVE" TRUTH!

YOU
ARE BOTH
"SOMETHING/SOMEBODY"
AND
"NOTHING/NOBODY!"

YOUR "I AM" IS
"NOTHING/NOBODY"
AND
EVERYTHING
AFTER
YOUR "I AM" IS
"SOMETHING/SOMEBODY!"

YOU ARE
"SOMETHING/SOMEBODY"
AS
THE PERSON
(BODY-MIND)!

YOU ARE
"NOTHING/NOBODY"
WITHOUT
THE PERSON
(BODY-MIND)!

BUT YOU STILL
"ARE!"

YOUR IDENTIFICATION AS THE PERSON (BODY-MIND) IS WHAT YOU 'THINK' YOU ARE!

YOUR IDENTIFICATION WITHOUT THE PERSON (BODY-MIND) IS WHAT YOU TRULY ARE!

ALL SPIRITUAL PRACTICES WORK TO "SHIFT" YOUR IDENTIFICATION FROM THE "RELATIVE" TO THE "ABSOLUTE!"

FROM BEING SOMETHING/SOMEBODY TO BEING NOTHING/NOBODY!

ALL SPIRITUAL PRACTICES REQUIRE EFFORT BEFORE THEY BECOME "EFFORTLESS!"

SHED EVERYTHING TO REVEAL NOTHING!

The Power Of Nothing

The POWER OF NOTHING!

INSTRUCTIONS BOOKLET

STEP 1:
Choose A Place Where You Can Spend At Least 30 Minutes Absoutely Alone & Undistrurbed!

STEP 2:
Choose A Comfortable Position To Sit In That Won't Require You To Move About!

You Need Not Be Still But Just Comfortable!

STEP 3:
As You Sit, Mentally Empty Your Mind Of All Thoughts!

Don't Touch Any Thoughts Of The Past, Present Or Future Of Your Entire Life!

Put All Those Thoughts Out Of Your Mind For The Time Being!

Empty Even The Thought Of 'What Next?'. Empty The Mind Until There Is No Thought!

Ensure That There Is No Mental Image Or Mental Voice In The Mind!

Have A Completely BLANK Mind!

STEP 4:
With A BLANK Mind, Now Mentally Drop The Awareness Of Your Body And The Surroundings!

Your Body Will Continue To Function Perfectly Fine Without Your Attention Directed Towards It!

STEP 5:
Observe That When There Is No Thought In The Mind AND You Have Mentally Dropped The Awareness Of The Body And Surroundings, There Is Nothing To Experience AND That YOU Are Still There!

There Is YOU & NOTHING!

STEP 6:
Observe This NOTHING With A Blank Mind. You'll Find That This 'NOTHING' Which Is Not A 'Thing' Still IS!

It Has Some Sort Of Issness, Existence Or Presence!

You Can't Say WHAT It Is BUT It IS There!

IT JUST IS!

We Don't Know What It Is But It IS!

Let's Call This Existence 'NOTHINGNESS" For The Time Being!

STEP 7:
This Nothingness Feels Like Space. Observe And You'll Find That It Is Everywhere! You Are Now 'Directly' Experiencing This Nothingness!

STEP 8:
Inquire Further Into This Nothingness With The Following Questions And Answer Them Through Your Direct Experience!

Does This Nothingness Have A Beginning, Middle Or Ending?
Does It Have A Shape, Size Or Form?
Can You See, Hear, Smell, Taste Or Touch It?
Does It Have A Color?
Is There Any Place Where It Is Not?
Did It Just Come Up Now?

Where Has This Nothingness
Been All This While?
Can It Ever Go Away?
Can You Get Rid Of It?

STEP 9:
Continue The Inquiry With
The Following Questions:
Was This Nothingness Ever Born?
Can It Be Affected By Disease
Or Old Age?
Is There Anything That Exists
Outside This Nothingness?
Does It Need To Become Rich
Or Famous?
Does It Need To Become
Enlightened?
Can You Do Anything 'To'
Or 'With' This Nothingness?
Can It Die?
When Your Body Dies Will
This Nothingness Still
Be There?

STEP 10:
Inquire Further Into This Nothingness:

Is There Any Distance Or Gap Between You and This Nothingness?
If There Is No Gap Between You And It, Then It Must Be YOU!
Is This Nothingness YOU?
If It Is YOU Then All The Previous Answers Are About YOU!

YOU Were Never Born, You Can Never Die, You Are Untouched By Pain & Suffering.
Observe That You Cannot 'Do' Anything To Or With This Nothingness. You Can Only 'BE' This Nothingness!
This NOTHINGNESS Is Your True Self/Brahman/Absolute Truth/Reality etc!

Everything 'Appears' Within This Nothingness!

This Nothingness Is Pure Existence, Pure Consciousness, Pure Bliss, Peace Itself, Love Itself Etc!

It Is Infinite, Formless And IMMORTAL And It Is YOU!

YOU Are Infinite, Formless, Non-Dual, Fearless And IMMORTAL!

YOUR True Nature/Identity/Self IS THIS NOTHING-NESS!

SOAK YOURSELF IN THIS 'NOTHING-NESS' UNTIL YOUR EGO DISSOLVES OR MERGES INTO IT!!!!

ABIDE "IN" THE NOTHING-NESS "AS" THE NOTHING-NESS!

SHRAVANAM. MANANAM. NIDHIDHYASANA!

LISTEN. UNDERSTAND. MEDITATE!

HEAR NOTHING. UNDERSTAND NOTHING. MEDITATE ON NOTHING!

ABOUT THE AUTHOR

Sukhdev Virdee was born and brought up in Nairobi, Kenya. Since childhood he was very inclined towards spirituality and music. After his studies he chose to take up music as a profession. He learnt how to play the keyboards and started performing live on stage at the age of nineteen. He later went to London and completed a BTEC in Music Production and Performance.

He later flew to Mumbai, India to pursue his dream of singing and composing music in the largest Indian Entertainment Industry. His debut pop-album became a chartbuster making him a popular household name in India and across the world. Mumbai became his home where he is known for his high energy live performances and this popularity took him to several countries across every continent on the planet to perform live for huge audiences.

A few more albums and singles followed after that. He was living the life that every young person looks up to even today. He had created a name for himself and enjoyed the name, fame and fortune that most singers dream of but never get to live. During all this he was totally oblivious of what life had in store for him in the coming years.

Just before his 40th birthday, when he was going through a rather rough patch in life, three of his friends gifted him the Bhagavad Gita out of the blue. These were friends that he met only occasionally and yet within two weeks three different people gifted him the Bhagavad Gita that would change his life completely. He read the Bhagavad Gita and felt Lord Krishna was speaking directly to him. It completely changed his outlook towards life as he followed the teachings in the Bhagavad Gita as best as he could.

Just over a year later, one fine morning after he woke up from his morning meditation and walked towards his temple in the house, his body completely froze and in an instant he had become one with the entire Universe. Time stood still and every particle of the entire Universe was alive and shining in bright golden light and he was the light. He was no longer limited to just his body or mind, he was everywhere at the same time and everything was one with him.

This Spiritual awakening experience turned his life upside down and inside out. All desires for anything worldly vanished, fear of death vanished, love and compassion for entire humanity and nature arose and he could feel and experience the Supreme Being in everything.

Not knowing exactly what had happened and what to do next, he sought out several resources before he was pointed towards the Upanishads that answered all his questions as to what had happened, what led to it and what to do after such an awakening.

After years of studying the Vedanta texts he is now an expert on non-dual Vedanta through not only intellectual and philosophical knowledge but most importantly with his own personal direct experience everyday.

He has put all his heart and soul into writing these books that include the highest knowledge of the Upanishads and his own direct experience and knowledge of the Supreme Being.

The books have been written with the absolute conviction that you, the reader, can realize your true immortal Universal Self too, that you are pure bliss and completely unaffected by all pain and suffering.

The promise of all spirituality is that one transcends pain and sorrow in this world, not that pain and sorrow don't come, but that the realized being is untouched by it. One realizes that their true nature is immortal, that they are one with the Universe. Would a being that realizes that he or she is one with the Universe ever want to accumulate anything in this world?

No, the True Saint or Sage who is Self-Realized makes do with only the very basic necessities required to live an honest decent life. They don't look to gain wealth, become famous, build an empire or any such sort of selfish activities.

Their main focus becomes serving humanity selflessly and uplifting others to help them realize their true nature so that they too can transcend suffering and realize their Oneness with the Universe. Sukhdev aims to do just that through his music, art and writing in the remaining days that he has left in this mortal body.

"I Am Consciousness"
6 Book Series
A Journey From Seeker
To Enlightened Master
Available As
E-books & Paperbacks
On Amazon & Other Digital Stores

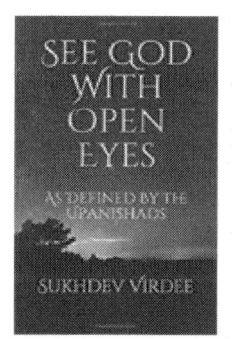

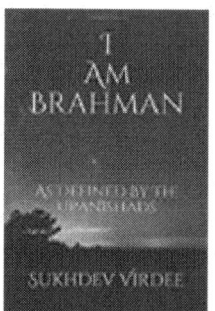

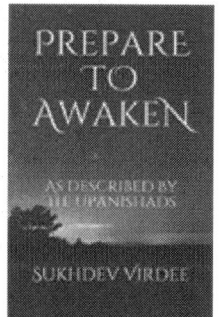

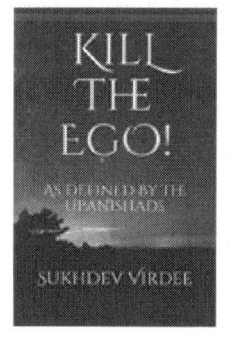

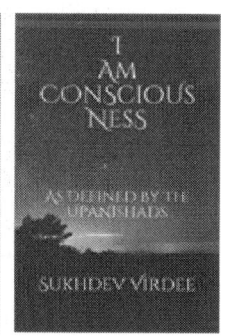

Available As
E-books & Paperbacks
On Amazon & Other Digital Stores

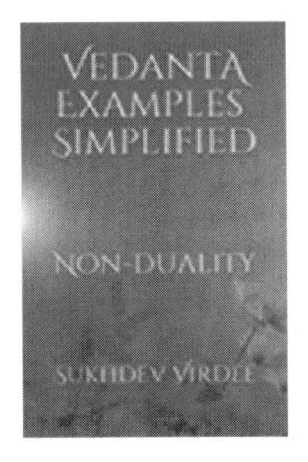

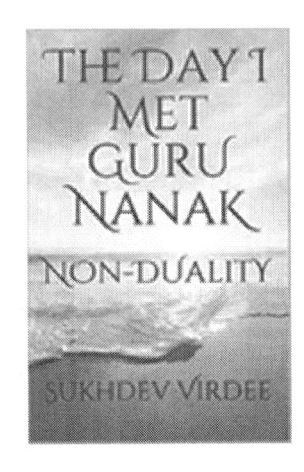

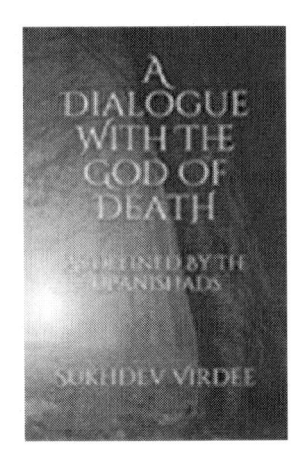

Printed in Great Britain
by Amazon